EDGE BOOKS

MONSTER HANDBOOKS

WEREWOLVES

The Truth Behind
HISTORY'S SCARIEST SHAPE-SHIFTERS

by Sean McCollum

Consultant:
David Gilmore, Professor of Anthropology
Stony Brook University, New York

CAPSTONE PRESS

Edge Books are published by Capstone Press,
1710 Roe Crest Drive, North Mankato, Minnesota 56003.
www.capstonepub.com

Library of Congress Cataloging-in-Publication Data
McCollum, Sean, author.
Werewolves : the truth behind history's scariest shape-shifters / by Sean McCollum.
pages cm.—(Edge books. Monster handbooks)
Summary: "Describes ancient history, medieval lore, and modern portrayals
of werewolves in today's popular culture"—Provided by publisher.
Audience: 8–12.
Audience: Grades 4–6.
Includes bibliographical references and index.
ISBN 978-1-4914-4251-7 (library binding)
ISBN 978-1-4914-4336-1 (paperback)
ISBN 978-1-4914-4312-5 (ebook PDF)
1. Werewolves—Juvenile literature. 2. Shapeshifting—Juvenile literature.
3. Werewolves in literature—Juvenile literature. I. Title.
GR830.W4M338 2016
398.24'54—dc23   2015001433

Editorial Credits
Aaron Sautter, editor; Bobbie Nuytten, designer; Gina Kammer, media researcher;
Laura Manthe, production specialist

Photo Credits
Alamy: © Ivy Close Images, 11, © Jeff Morgan 10, 8, © Lordprice Collection, 23, ©
Pictorial Press Ltd, 25; Corbis: © Bettmann, 24; Dreamstime: © Mccool, (bottom) 21;
Getty Images: De Agostini Picture Library, 14, Syfy, 28; Glow Images: Heritage Images/
Ann Ronan Pictures, 19; Granger, NYC, (top) 17; Mary Evans Picture Library, 7; Newscom:
akg-images, 12, Album/AMERICAN INTERNATIONAL PICTURES, 26; Shutterstock:
andreiuc88, cover, 1, ARTEMENKO VALENTYN, 18, breaker213, 5, Brianito, 10, 30,
Debbie Steinhausser, (bottom) 27, Larysa Ray, 4, Lasha Kilasonia, (Earth map) 9, Michael
Vigliotti, (bottom) 17, Michal Jurkowski, (middle) 21, Nyord, cover, 1, Richard Peterson, (top)
21, SeDmi, 20, Shukaylova Zinaida, 13

Design Elements
Shutterstock: Ensuper (grunge background), Larysa Ray (grunge frames), Slava Gerj (grunge
scratched background)

Printed in China by Nordica
0415/CA21500562
032015   008844NORDF15

Table of Contents

POWER OF THE WOLF

As a full moon rises above the forest, fog creeps between the black shapes of trees. Soon an eerie howl rises above the mist, "Ah-WOO-oooo!" When we hear that sound in the movies it can mean only one thing—a werewolf is on the prowl!

Werewolves aren't real, but long ago many people believed they were. Tales about them have existed for thousands of years wherever wolves have roamed. These fierce monsters have gone through many changes throughout history. Beliefs about werewolves in ancient times were very different from how they're seen today.

In the past these monsters often appeared as bloodthirsty predators. They prowled through the night and attacked anything that moved. However, in modern stories werewolves are often the unfortunate victims of a **curse**. Sometimes they're even seen as heroes that fight to protect humans. But no matter how werewolves are portrayed, these **shape-shifters** have long had a powerful grip on people's imaginations.

curse—an evil spell meant to harm or punish someone
shape-shifter—a creature that is able to change its physical form

Chapter 1
SHAPE-SHIFTERS FROM LONG AGO

People have long been fascinated by the idea of humans changing into other creatures. Thousands of years ago ancient cultures often created tales featuring such shape-shifters.

Shape-Shifters in Ancient Greece

Shape-shifting was a common theme in stories from ancient Greece. Greek poets often told fantastic tales featuring half-human creatures such as mermaids and **centaurs**. Many ancient Greek stories also tell of how the gods changed people into dogs, deer, birds, and other creatures.

The idea of people changing form wasn't limited to ancient Greek poets. The famous Greek historian Herodotus (hih-ROD-uh-tuhs) also passed along a story about shape-changing people. During his travels Herodotus learned about the distant Neuri tribe. He was told that the Neuri people could turn into wolves once every year. However, although Herodotus recorded this legend in his writings, he didn't believe the story himself.

centaur—a creature with the head and chest of a human and the body of a horse

FACT: In one ancient Greek tale, King Lycaon (lie-KAY-ahn) nearly tricks Zeus, the king of the gods, into eating human flesh. When Zeus learns about Lycaon's trick, he punishes the wicked king by turning him into a wolf.

Rome's Wolf Warriors

Rome was famous for its powerful army, which included specially trained "wolf" warriors. These soldiers wore the skins and skulls of wolves in order to "become the wolf" during battle. The Romans didn't believe these soldiers actually became wolves. But the **ritual** was thought to give them wolflike strength and **cunning** in battle.

When Roman armies invaded central and northern Europe betwen 58 and 53 BC, they had a surprise waiting for them. They met Germanic people who also had fierce wolf-skin warriors. Reports state that these men were especially ferocious in battle. The Romans were impressed by these warriors. They even hired some of them to fight for Rome!

ritual—a ceremony involving a set of religious actions

cunning—being sneaky or clever at tricking people

FACT: One Roman tale tells of two brothers, Romulus and Remus, who were raised by a wolf. The young men supposedly had wolflike qualities such as cleverness, boldness, and "wolf spirit." These mythical leaders are remembered as the founders of the great city of Rome.

SHAPE-SHIFTERS AROUND THE WORLD

Ancient cultures believed in a variety of shape-shifting creatures. Religious leaders and healers known as shamans were often thought to magically become other creatures. People believed that some shamans could even send their spirits into animals to control them.

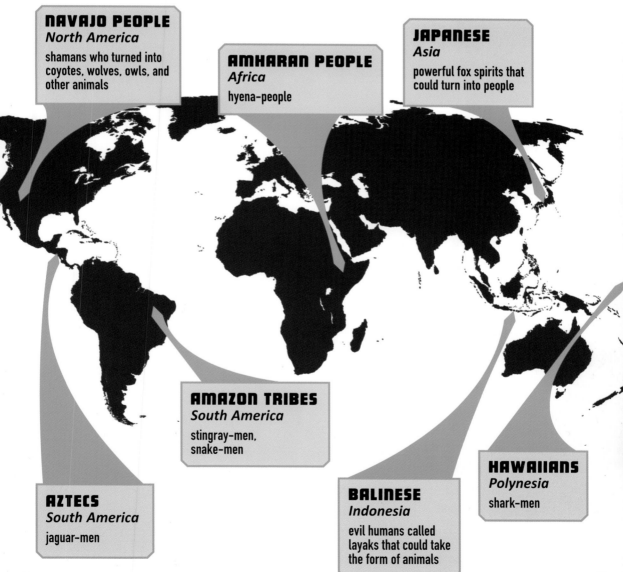

NAVAJO PEOPLE
North America
shamans who turned into coyotes, wolves, owls, and other animals

AMHARAN PEOPLE
Africa
hyena-people

JAPANESE
Asia
powerful fox spirits that could turn into people

AMAZON TRIBES
South America
stingray-men, snake-men

HAWAIIANS
Polynesia
shark-men

AZTECS
South America
jaguar-men

BALINESE
Indonesia
evil humans called layaks that could take the form of animals

Chapter 2
THE WEREWOLVES OF EUROPE

About 1,200 years ago, bands of Viking raiders swept across the British Isles and northern Europe. These warriors were reportedly so ferocious that people called them "wolves." Some of them even wore wolf-skins and wolf-heads. Soon a new name was whispered among their victims—"werewolf." It meant "man-wolf" or "outlaw-wolf" and described a person who could become a fierce killer.

FACT: Some stories from the 1500s described people who didn't actually turn into wolves. They looked normal but were said to have the strength and vicious nature of a wolf.

Werewolves in the Middle Ages

During the Middle Ages (about AD 500 to 1450), poems and tales about werewolves often appeared across Europe. These **medieval** stories sometimes showed werewolves as rational and gentle, or even as the heroes. The heroic creatures were often people who had been cursed to become wolflike creatures but still tried to help others. However, werewolves in most tales were terrifying monsters. They were violent beasts that often attacked and killed innocent people.

medieval—having to do with the period of history between AD 500 and 1450

In the tale "William of Palermo," a friendly werewolf carries a young prince into the forest to protect him from his wicked uncle.

Becoming a Werewolf

Medieval **lore** shows a wide range of beliefs about how someone could become a werewolf. In some tales people could change their form by magic. They might cast a spell, drink a magic potion, or use a magical object to become a werewolf. German **peasants** often believed someone could put on a wolf-skin belt and say some magic words to become a wolf.

In several medieval tales people make a deal with the Devil. These people sell their souls to receive the speed, strength, and violent nature of a wolf.

In Serbia it was said that drinking rainwater from a wolf's footprint could turn someone into a werewolf. And in southern France, a few people were thought to have an uncontrollable urge to jump into a pond during a full moon. The person then climbed out of the water in the shape of a wolf.

lore—traditional knowledge and beliefs about a subject

peasant—a poor and uneducated person who works on a farm

FACT: The idea that werewolves changed form during a full moon was first written about in the 1200s. But this didn't become a popular part of werewolf lore until the early 1900s.

Werewolves on Trial

During the Middle Ages people across Europe had great fear of the **supernatural**. Books and pamphlets described many stories about monsters that harmed the innocent. These stories often caused people in towns and villages to panic. They sometimes jumped to conclusions about suspected werewolves, often with tragic results.

For example, if a farmer found one of his animals had been killed violently, he might suspect a wolf. But if no wolf was caught, he and others might think the killer was a werewolf instead. The hunt would soon be on for someone to blame. Perhaps a wandering stranger would be accused of being the killer. Other times a person with a mental illness was thought to be the monster.

In France, Germany, and other parts of Europe, mobs were sometimes formed to hunt down werewolves. When the suspects were captured, they were put on trial. These innocent people were often tortured until they confessed to being a werewolf. Then they were usually put to death.

supernatural—something that cannot be given an ordinary explanation

THE WEREWOLF OF BEDBURG

In the 1580s the German village of Bedburg experienced several unexplained killings. Cattle were torn apart as though a vicious animal had attacked them. Then villagers began disappearing and were later found dead.

The villagers believed that a bloodthirsty wolf was on the prowl. They organized a hunt with dogs and chased a wolf until they had it cornered. The hunters said they saw the wolf change into a local farmer named Peter Stubbe. Stubbe was put on trial as a werewolf and was found guilty. His wife and daughter were also found guilty of helping him. All three were put to death.

Chapter 3
DEFENSE AGAINST WEREWOLVES

At one time tracking down a werewolf was like hunting any other animal. Werewolf hunters didn't use weapons believed to have magical powers. They instead used normal weapons such as swords, bows, and arrows to hunt and kill werewolves.

The Wolf of Ansbach

One such werewolf hunt took place in Germany in 1685. A wolf near the town of Ansbach had killed several farm animals. It had also reportedly attacked women and children. Rumors soon spread that the wolf was really the town's dead mayor. Some people thought that he had come back to life as a werewolf.

Armed with dogs, pitchforks, and clubs, some local hunters trapped the wolf in a well and killed it. But the dead wolf didn't change back to human form. To save their reputation, the hunters decided to make the wolf look like a real werewolf. They cut off its **muzzle** and put a mask over its face. They also put a wig on its head and dressed it in human clothes. They then hung the wolf in the town square to show everyone that they had killed the werewolf.

muzzle—an animal's nose, mouth, and jaws

This gruesome tale shows how people once believed that werewolves could be killed with regular weapons. However, that belief wouldn't last. These mythical monsters would soon become much harder to kill.

FACT: Wolves in England had been hunted to extinction by the end of the 1600s. As a result, werewolf tales in England were rare.

Changing the Shape-Shifter

By the 1800s werewolves in many stories were becoming scarier and more dangerous. People began to believe that magic was the best defense against these violent killers.

Many people thought magic could turn werewolves back into human beings. One method involved calling out a werewolf's human name three times. This supposedly forced the creature to immediately change back to its human form.

Farmers in Germany claimed that iron and steel had magical effects on werewolves. Tossing an iron or steel object over one of these monsters was thought to force it to become human again. However, the person's eyes were said to glow like a wolf's for a while afterward.

In many stories a werewolf's wife or husband had the ability to stop it. One German tale tells of a farmer who saw a red-haired werewolf running through a field. He shouted out his wife's name and she changed back immediately.

Another story from Denmark describes a man who knew he would soon turn into a werewolf. He told his wife that if any animal attacked her she should use her apron to defend herself. Before long a wolf appeared and the woman hit it with her apron. The wolf bit off a piece of the apron and ran away. Soon her husband returned with the piece of apron in his mouth. The man told his wife that he had been a werewolf. But she had helped break the curse and he was now just a normal man.

Some old tales described "wolf charmers" as people who used musical magic spells to control both regular wolves and werewolves.

monkshood, also known as wolfsbane

Magical Werewolf Weapons

In many tales werewolves couldn't be cured or changed back into humans. The monsters instead had to be killed. However, by the 1800s werewolves in most stories had grown very powerful. Regular weapons like pitchforks and arrows could no longer pierce their hides. And normal bullets just bounced off of them. Sharp-edged weapons like axes or swords might work, but only if they were made of iron.

To solve this problem, werewolf lore began to include magical weapons that could kill the beasts. In some parts of Europe, plants with magical properties were said to be the best weapons. A stake from alder wood could pierce a werewolf's magical hide and kill it. The poisonous flower known as **wolfsbane** was also thought to be an effective werewolf weapon.

wolfsbane—a poisonous plant with purple hoodlike flowers

People in Germany thought that **inherited** silver could harm werewolves. For example, a bullet made from an inherited silver button could kill or wound a werewolf. People could also use a parent's silver dagger or knife to kill these monsters.

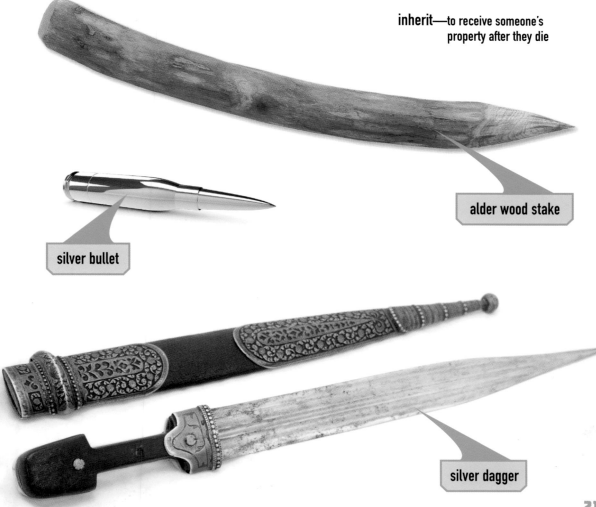

inherit—to receive someone's property after they die

alder wood stake

silver bullet

silver dagger

Chapter 4
WILD ABOUT WEREWOLVES

A pair of hikers walk along a dark and secluded forest path. Suddenly they hear a wolf's howl. They run away, but just when they think they're safe, the werewolf attacks! Then somewhere in the darkened movie theater, a terrified person screams.

Many people enjoy being frightened by monsters and scary stories. Since the 1900s few scary creatures have been more popular than werewolves. Rather than being half-forgotten characters in old folk tales, werewolves became superstars in fiction stories and film.

Werewolf Literature

Werewolves began their makeover in the mid-1800s. Writers took the old tales about the monsters and turned them into stories that everybody could enjoy. Stories featuring werewolves, vampires, and other monsters soon became best sellers. *The Man-Wolf* (1831), "A Story of a Weir-Wolf" (1846), and *Wagner, the Wehr-Wolf* (1846) are just a few examples.

By the end of the 1800s, werewolf tales were more popular than ever. People enjoyed the thrills and chills of how werewolves were created and how to fight them. But soon the invention of film would cause their popularity to explode.

The Book of Were-Wolves *by Sabine Baring-Gould was first published in 1865. It is filled with folktales and illustrations of werewolves.*

Werewolves Go To Hollywood

Werewolves got their big break in American movies during the mid-1900s. Hollywood released one of its first werewolf films, *Werewolf of London*, in 1935. But in 1941 *The Wolf Man* really got

audiences shrieking. People loved it. They finally got to see just how exciting and scary werewolves could be. Two years later werewolves thrilled people again in the film *Frankenstein Meets the Wolf Man*.

Hollywood films changed many of the rules for werewolves. In the past werewolves had often been people who chose to become monsters. Hunting and killing them was also fairly simple. But Hollywood's new rules made werewolves more terrifying. They had supernatural strength and speed. And they were difficult to kill. Bullets and other non-magical weapons could not harm them.

FACT: For *The Wolf Man* (1941), actor Lon Chaney Jr. sat still for nine hours while artists put on his makeup.

HOLLYWOOD WEREWOLF LORE

In the mid-1900s, Hollywood established several new rules for werewolves in the movies. Some of these include:

➤ werewolves change shape under the light of a full moon

➤ werewolves walk on two legs like humans

➤ werewolves have supernatural strength and speed and are not harmed by bullets or normal weapons

➤ in human form werewolves can be good people, but they usually become violent killers in werewolf form

➤ a victim who is bitten or scratched by a werewolf will later become a werewolf

➤ wolfsbane can weaken or even kill werewolves

➤ weapons made of silver, such as bullets and knives, can injure or kill werewolves

The film I Was a Teenage Werewolf was a big hit with audiences in 1957.

The Popular Werewolf

The popularity of *The Wolf Man* revealed how much people enjoyed being scared by these make-believe monsters. The popularity of werewolves continued to climb. During the 1950s Hollywood made several more movies featuring everyone's favorite wild monsters. Werewolves were soon seen everywhere, from movies to comic books, kids' toys, and TV shows. Werewolves were also a popular costume choice on Halloween. Kids wore werewolf masks, furry gloves with plastic claws, and plastic werewolf fangs.

Werewolves Shift Again

In the 1980s and 1990s, werewolves became easier to like. In several stories they were shown as victims of a terrible curse. Werewolves even became heroes in some stories. They resisted the urge to kill and tried to avoid people when in wolf form.

This shift in werewolves in popular culture may have reflected changes in people's feelings about real wolves. People feared and hated wild wolves for hundreds of years. But in the 1970s people became more aware of wolves' important role in nature. When wolves nearly became extinct in much of North America, it was decided to include them in the U.S. Endangered Species Act. This 1973 law states that endangered animals can't be hunted or killed by humans.

Today wolf populations have bounced back. Thousands of wolves roam in the wild in North America.

Werewolves of Today and Tomorrow

Today werewolves show up in almost every form of entertainment. These creatures have changed throughout history, and today's monsters are no different. In many recent stories, wolf-men and wolf-women can transform whenever they wish—no full moon is required. Sometimes they become four-footed creatures, as in the *Twilight* books and movies. In other stories they may change into a human-wolf **hybrid**. People also no longer need to be bitten by a werewolf to become one. Sometimes these creatures are born into werewolf families or "packs." Being a werewolf is just a part of who they are.

Whether they have new abilities or use their strength to protect the innocent, werewolves continue to surprise audiences. In this way they continue to be true to werewolf legends of ancient days. These popular monsters are constantly shifting, in their character as well as their shape.

hybrid—a plant or animal that has traits from two different species

Transforming into a werewolf is often shown to be very painful in modern films and TV shows.

WEREWOLVES IN FILMS, TV, AND BOOKS

TITLE	MEDIA	CHARACTER	GOOD OR BAD
Werewolf of London (1935)	film	Wilfred Glendon	good person / bad wolf
The Wolf Man (1941)	film	Larry Talbot	good person / bad wolf
I Was a Teenage Werewolf (1957)	film	Tony Rivers	good person / bad wolf
The Curse of the Werewolf (1961)	film	Leon Corledo	good person / bad wolf
Teen Wolf (1985)	film	Scott Howard	good person/good wolf
The Monster Squad (1987)	film	Wolfman	good person / bad wolf
Buffy the Vampire Slayer (1997–2003)	TV	Daniel "Oz" Osbourne	good person / bad wolf
Harry Potter series (1997–2007)	novels	Fenrir Greyback Remus Lupin	bad person / bad wolf good person / bad wolf
Twilight series (2005–2008)	novels	Jacob Black	good person / good wolf
The Boy Who Cried Werewolf (2010)	TV movie	Jordan Sands	good person / good wolf
Grimm (2011–present)	TV	Monroe	good person / good wolf

GLOSSARY

centaur (SEN-tor)—a creature with the head and chest of a human and the body of a horse

cunning (KUN-ing)—being sneaky or clever at tricking people

curse (KURS)—an evil spell meant to harm or punish someone

hybrid (HYE-brid)—a plant or animal that has traits from two different species

inherit (in-HAIR-it)—to receive someone's property after they die

lore (LOHR)—traditional knowledge and beliefs about a subject

medieval (MEE-dee-vuhl)—having to do with the period of history between AD 500 and 1450

muzzle (MUHZ-uhl)—an animal's nose, mouth, and jaws

peasant (PEZ-uhnt)—a poor and uneducated person who works on a farm

ritual (RICH-oo-uhl)—a ceremony involving a set of religious actions

shape-shifter (SHAYP SHIF-tuhr)—a creature that is able to change its physical form

supernatural (soo-pur-NACH-ur-uhl)—something that cannot be given an ordinary explanation

wolfsbane (WOLFS-bayn)—a poisonous plant with purple hoodlike flowers

READ MORE

Bingham, Jane. *Vampires and Werewolves.* Solving Mysteries with Science. Chicago: Raintree, 2014.

Lestrade, Ursula. *The Werewolf Hunter's Guide.* Monster Tracker. Mankato, Minn.: Sea-to-Sea, 2012.

O'Hearn, Michael. *Vampires vs. Werewolves: Battle of the Bloodthirsty Beasts*. Monster Wars. Mankato, Minn.: Capstone Press, 2012.

INTERNET SITES

FactHound offers a safe, fun way to find Internet sites related to this book. All of the sites on FactHound have been researched by our staff.

Here's all you do:

Visit *www.facthound.com*

Type in this code: 9781491442517

Check out projects, games and lots more at
www.capstonekids.com

INDEX